THE DEATH
of DEMOCRACY

THE DEATH
of DEMOCRACY

by A Witness

REGENT PRESS
Berkeley, California

Copyright © 2020 Regent Press

Sixth Printing

[paperback]
ISBN 13: 978-1-58790-444-8
ISBN 10: 1-58790-444-6

[e-book]
ISBN 13: 978-1-58790-445-5
ISBN 10: 1-58790-445-4

Library of Congress Control Number: 2018942139

Manufactured in the U.S.A.
Regent Press
Berkeley, CA
www.regentpress.net

The typestyle used in this book is Adobe Garamond.

To those who once fought
to maintain our democracies

CONTENTS

INTRODUCTION

This is neither fiction nor fantasy. It is a description of events as they actually happened.

The death of democracy came quietly and unexpectedly in the year 2020. No one expected the end to come so quickly, although now looking back all the warning signs were there.

Within the early years of the twenty-first century the forces of democracy died a painful, slow death in Russia, Venezuela, Poland, Egypt, and many other nations. But because of what we considered our long and stable democratic tradition in the United States, we thought our democracy was safe.

Until now.

I write this clandestinely and away from the prying eyes of those who have removed our democratic institutions and destroyed the functioning of our legislature, courts, press, and every other safeguard we once took for granted to maintain human liberty.

In 1935 Sinclair Lewis warned in his novel *It Can't Happen Here* that democracy is fragile and vulnerable to destruction by legitimately elected leaders who claim that only they can overturn difficult economic conditions. They then use their positions to impose dictatorial powers. Before, during, and since that time there have been numerous politicians in many countries who have followed that pattern. Yet few of us ever expected that democracy's end would come in our lifetime.

In countries of the Far East, such as China, there has been a tradition of top-down dictatorial government for thousands of years. The Maoist Revolution of 1949 that promised greater equality for the masses chased the dictatorial government of Chiang Kai-shek to Taiwan and replaced it with another dictatorship. Despite what seemed like years of slow progress toward greater human rights, the President of China now has been declared President for Life. Dictatorial rule still exists in many smaller Eastern countries such as Vietnam and Myanmar. The President of the Philippines, which once was a democracy, routinely kills those with whose politics or lifestyles he disagrees.

In Central and South America, there were countless revolutions against the ruling classes since the subjugation of the native populations by the Spanish and Portuguese 500 years ago. The result was a series of corrupt governments. Venezuela elected Hugo Chavez as a reformer in 1998, who eventually suspended the rule of law, packed the courts, and ended presidential term limits. Brazil, among other Latin American countries, is embroiled in chronic corruption, with the huge gap between the wealthiest and poorest little changed since its earliest days.

In Eastern Europe the concept of Father Russia has returned to the country of the Tsars. A brief failed experiment with democracy following the collapse of the Soviet Union in 1991 ended with the ascension of Vladimir Putin to the presidency in 2000. Many nations of the previous Soviet Bloc that seemed on the verge of democratic revolution, such as Hungary and Poland, now have installed a renewed autocracy.

In The Middle East, the Arab Spring of 2011 that gave hope to Egypt has regressed once again to dictatorship. Libya, freed from the whims of Muammar Gaddafi after Western powers helped overthrow him, had its aspirations of democracy crushed amidst ongoing internal strife. Syria has suffered hundreds of thousands of deaths in its civil war. And in Turkey, a once promising democracy, its people now suffer under autocratic domination.

After the Great Recession that began in the United States and Europe in 2008, a new "populist" surge appealed to those who were economically stagnating. The emphasis of "populist" leaders was whom to blame for economic problems – often members of a targeted political party or those who look different from the majority. But "populism" actually was a power grab by those who represented the interests of a disenfranchised part of the population, not the people as a whole. It undermined real democracy. In England, France, Germany and Italy, populism affected elections that failed to provide mandates for democratic principles. In the United States, Our Leader became President in 2017, despite losing the majority vote.

History has shown that democracies rarely last more than a couple of hundred years. The democracy of Athens was in place from about 600 to 400 BCE, with a number of regressions into tyranny during that period. There were elements of democracy in ancient Rome and parts of Europe during the Middle Ages and Renaissance. There even was an effort among native tribes in North America to establish a Great Law of Peace run by consensus. In our day, the countries of Western Europe and the Americas now have failed to maintain their democracies after this same period of about two hundred years.

The following pages are a chronicle of how those most responsible for sustaining democracies – the people of those societies themselves – abandoned their roles as its guardians and allowed it to be overthrown, perhaps for all time.

DEMOCRACY'S BIRTH

OUR EARLIEST ANCESTORS made decisions essential for their survival within the family and tribe. Communication usually was successful because people in small groups can interact directly. Those which used group decision-making about, for example, where, what and when to hunt, were most likely to survive. Each individual benefitted when the overall decision-making process was successful, so input from members and submission to the group process improved their chances of survival. This model for democratic decision making is a part of the genetic makeup of every human being.

Because of the limits of experience and views of each individual, collaboration to arrive at the best path forward increased the chances of survival for everyone. Cooperation among a broad group of community members – rather than just submission to the decisions of only one leader – were likely to lead to the most successful actions to benefit the group.

As tribes grew and expanded into nations, democratic decision making became more difficult. This was due to the increasing distance between people and their leaders. The democratic elements in early societies diminished as dominant leaders made more of the major decisions. Customs and rules became more established to provide guidance, rather than decision making geared to each new situation.

The Greeks were among the earliest civilizations to renew the idea of democratic decision making. Major government decisions were made by citizens in the period of Athenian democracy.

This was an agrarian society where many farmers accumulated substantial debt to sustain themselves and their families in years when crops failed. Borrowing during lean years led to a widening division between the rich and poor, sometimes resulting in slavery for those in debt. Their leader at the beginning of this period, Solon, created a law that allowed Athenian farmers to reduce or cancel their debts. The result was a reversal of vast inequality, and greater prosperity for everyone. The state became more viable as the economy became more stable. Athens became a state where "the people" authorized the laws and their implementation. The word democracy is based on the Greek term that means "government by the People."

The Athenians were proud of their democracy. Pericles, their leader and general, spoke about its benefits after a battle with their rival Sparta:

Our constitution does not copy the laws of neighboring states; we are rather a pattern to others than imitators ourselves. Its administration favors the many instead of the few; this is why it is called a democracy. If we look to the laws, they afford equal justice to all in their private differences; if no social standing, advancement in public life falls to reputation for capacity, class considerations not being allowed to interfere with merit; nor again does poverty bar the way, if a man is able to serve the state, he is not hindered by the obscurity of his condition.

Although Athenian democracy was revolutionary for its time, only about 10% of Athenians — those who were male citizens — were able to participate directly.

The Greeks also emphasized individual achievement in their democracy. They invented the Olympic Games and trained their children to compete in a number of competitions. But they also emphasized the importance of discussing and identifying their core values in schools such as those set up by Plato and Aristotle. Within their city-states there was the same conflict that has existed in every human social structure – how to balance individual needs with those of society. Socrates was executed for teaching his followers to think about what really is important in life, which threatened those who believed that such thinking undermined the state.

After the Greek civilization declined, there were democratic elements in a number of Western civilizations, including that of Rome, where Julius Caesar was assassinated for trying to establish himself as "Emperor for Life." That event marked the beginning of the deterioration of Rome's peaceful political order.

In 1215, a group of English nobles forced King John to sign the Magna Carta, which removed his absolute authority and required him to consult with them about taxation. This was a key moment in an uneven move toward greater democracy in the Western world. In the meantime the Eastern world remained under autocratic rule.

In the 1700s a group of writers who represented a new wave of thought emerged in Western Europe. These Enlightenment writers – including Locke, Rousseau, and Voltaire – ignited the imaginations of prominent citizens, including leaders in the thirteen New World colonies who considered themselves oppressed under the English Crown. The essential message of the Enlightenment writers was that the purpose of government is to enhance the freedom of those who live under it. According to John Locke:

The end of law is not to abolish or restrain, but to preserve and enlarge freedom. For in all the states of created beings capable of law, where there is no law, there is no freedom.

In declaring independence from England in 1776 the leaders of the American Revolution stated that their intent was to preserve "Life, Liberty and the Pursuit of Happiness" for people who lived in the thirteen colonies. Only about half of the colonists were originally in favor of the revolution, which was hard fought and almost lost, but many eventually saw the advantages of the newly established democratic system. The Declaration of Independence was a statement of the Revolution's leaders about their desire to overthrow oppression. But after eleven years under a weak Articles of Confederation it became clear that a strong constitution was needed to solidify the direction of the young country. Thus they created the first written constitution of any nation.

It took four months of intense negotiation to write the US Constitution. The founders discovered that creating a forward-looking statement that included the principles upon which the country was to function was much more challenging than declaring their independence. Because they were aware that they had created an imperfect document that would need revision over time, they wrote the amendment process into the text. Their intent was summarized at the very beginning:

We the People of the United States, in Order to form a more perfect Union, establish Justice, insure domestic Tranquility, provide for the common defense, promote the general Welfare, and secure the Blessings of Liberty to ourselves and our Posterity, do ordain and establish this Constitution for the United States of America.

Yet again, as in ancient Greece, only a small minority of the three million individuals who made up the new country actually was able to participate in that democracy. Women, slaves, Native Americans, and of course children were excluded from the vote.

Soon afterwards, in 1789, the revolution in France overthrew its monarchy, largely inspired by the American Revolution. But unlike the United States, its leaders were not able to agree on a stable direction for their nation. Instead they fluctuated between republic and monarchy for 80 years.

Since that time democracy has been tried in over 100 nations in many different forms. Some countries have strived to establish genuinely representative democracies – Western European countries, Japan, and some in Africa and Latin America. Many, such as China and Russia, despite constitutions that promise democracy, cannot seriously be considered democratic. Thus the laws of a country are less likely to ensure democracy than the commitment of its people to democratic principles, a commitment that has greatly faded across the Western World in recent years.

There is an impulse within every human being to cooperate and recognize the validity of other human beings. This is how the earliest democratic societies came about and how the human race, by taking advantage of ideas from the best minds available, initially succeeded. Our earliest ancestors were able to work together for the common good because they knew that their most important interests were served by a group effort to support the survival of everyone. Customs and rules were established that governed each individual as a member of society.

The democracies of ancient Greece – and then the other Western countries – were attempts to return to that principle of cooperation.

But there also is another impulse within human beings – to compete with others and defeat them for individual survival. Successful societies find a way to sublimate that impulse for the good of the whole – in games, for example. Prioritizing the interests of the individual over those of the group ultimately led to democracy's demise. We began to believe that our interests were separate from others and emphasized our differences more than what we had in common. We grouped ourselves with those of similar race, religion, gender, or political belief in opposition to others, rather than emphasizing common goals and working toward them. But race, religion, gender, and other identifiers only are a small part of who we really are.

Some have said that the very idea of democracy was naïve and that people by nature cannot overcome their tendency to compete at the expense of others. But some – including the visionaries who founded the United States – believed that to have a society that works for any of us we must create a shared vision and work together to move in that direction via universal respect. Recent events seem to show that those who believe that democracy is a failed experiment are correct.

HOW WE SUCCEEDED

Since its inception, democracy, or "government by the People," has moved forward where there was relative equality, and has regressed where there was inequality. When the bulk of the population contributes their talents and abilities for the benefit of the whole, the society and economy thrives, but the more that the contributions of individuals to the whole are held back, the more a society regresses.

After the American Revolution, democratic ideals spread slowly around the world. These ideals already had been making their way in Western

Europe by the mid-1700s, thanks to the Enlightenment writers and a series of scientific discoveries and inventions that made life easier for many. But the resulting Industrial Revolution also led to great misery for the multitudes who worked long hours in factories for low pay, including their children. Agriculture still was the occupation of many for whom farming was a way of barely scratching out a living.

Alexis De Tocqueville, a Frenchman who visited the United States in 1830, made observations about the new nation that he related in his classic ***Democracy in America***. He was impressed with the vibrancy and energy he saw all around him but was concerned by the lack of reflection of many Americans who could barely discuss the democratic principles of their own nation. His impression was that Americans, while enjoying their freedoms, were in danger of losing them due to a limited understanding of what made them free. He also was concerned about the lack of extension of these freedoms by the white majority to oppressed minorities:

I know of no people who have established schools so numerous and efficacious, places of public worship better suited to the wants of the inhabitants, or roads kept in better repair....[But also] *I know of no country in which there is so little independence of mind and real freedom of discussion as in America..... [And] I attribute the small number of distinguished men in political life to the ever increasing despotism of the majority in the United States.*

During the 1800s slavery was banned by all major democracies, starting with France, then England, and then the US after a devastating civil war. Serfdom, akin to slavery, remained in Russia until its 1917 revolution. Slavery, however, has continued in some African nations, such as Chad and Congo, to this day.

By the end of the 1800s there was a widening gap between the wealthiest and those at the lower end of the economic scale in countries that considered themselves democratic. A struggle for better working conditions took place throughout the Western world. In the US, incidents such as the Haymarket riot of 1886 and the Pullman strike of 1894 personified this struggle. Labor unions formed which at times were opposed violently by factory owners, but eventually unions became essential bargaining units for raising the wages of workers and providing benefits such as limited working hours and improved health benefits.

As the world moved into the twentieth century greater rights were won for laborers in Western nations, with wages and benefits continuing to increase. Economic flow also improved as people were able to afford more products that eased their lives. Areas under Western domination, like India, also experienced progress. Inventions that made farming easier, such as the reaper, improved agricultural productivity. Innovations in transportation such as the railroad made it easier for people to get around. By the early 1900s the telephone, automobile, and electric light bulb – all the breakthroughs of Western democracies – eased the lives of millions. But in the countries of the East up until about 1900, with their top-down style of government, there was very little inventiveness or progress that positively affected the lives of the average person.

The scourges of disease and childhood mortality also lessened in the West. The recognition of better hygiene as a necessary accompaniment to health became more widespread. Inoculations for tuberculosis and polio greatly reduced these diseases, and innovations such as penicillin made bacterial infections less likely to kill.

In the United States the benefits and freedoms of democracy created a booming economy for ethnic majorities, who enjoyed increasing prosperity, while often leaving behind minorities such as immigrants, blacks and Native Americans. Yet serious economic downturns – the results of an extreme boom and bust economy – occurred with regularity every twenty years or so.

The First World War that began in 1914

resulted from the assassination of an Austrian noble by an anarchist who was deeply dissatisfied with what he saw as the great class divide. After that war ended, oppression of the Germans by the winning European nations such as England, France, Russia, and Italy created great resentment, eventually leading to the Second World War.

Women gained the right to vote in the US in 1920, then in the UK and France later in the century. Women also moved toward greater workplace equality in most Western nations from this time forward, but full workplace equality continued to be a struggle. Women headed the governments in Israel, Germany, Great Britain and Brazil in the twentieth and twenty-first centuries

By 1929 there still was a huge divide between the wealthiest individuals and the rest of the population in all Western democracies. Those at the top rode at the crest of a wave of prosperity, fueled by a stock market that seemed like it never would drop. People seemed to forget the periodic panics that had happened in 1772, 1792, 1819, 1837, 1857, 1893, and 1907. A gradually larger percent of the population invested their funds in stocks, assuming that they could only go one way. At that point the market was based largely on speculation rather than on a realistic expression of corporate profitability. Then the bubble burst and by 1930 the economy sped quickly downwards, leading to 25% unemployment and the destruction of large fortunes, small investments, and the demise of many banks.

One result was the Glass-Steagall Act, passed by the US Congress in 1933, that outlawed speculation by banks in investments with the money of their customers. It at last brought the democratic principle of protection of the average citizen into the nation's financial fabric. This law protected people in the US – and most of the world – for 66 years from practices that had led to a series of economic downturns.

Another result was the Social Security Act of 1933 which mandated that workers put a small percent of their earnings – matched by employers –

into a fund to be redeemed on retirement.

After World War II the Western nations – plus some in the East such as Japan – experienced record economic growth because they at last learned the importance of cooperation. The economic power and training capacity of the United States was unleashed to help the victorious and defeated nations alike lift themselves and participate in a vibrant world economy. The incomes of most individuals in the democratic countries greatly improved due to increased economic flow within and between their nations beginning in 1945.

European countries were primarily racially homogeneous during that period, but racial strife in the United States created an inequality that did not lift all boats. Discrimination, particularly against blacks in the South, remained rampant, despite the promises of the US Constitution. The civil rights activism of the 1960s resulted in violent confrontations between those who wanted change and those who sought to maintain the status quo of segregation, smaller pay and menial work for minorities.

Decisions by the US Supreme Court banning racial discrimination beginning in 1954 eventually forced the federal government to begin enforcing the democratic principles of the Constitution. But those who felt threatened by progress toward greater equality – both racial and economic – continued to hold on to their resentment and do their best to block progress. In Western Europe many who had become accustomed to racial homogeneity were alarmed by new waves of immigrants from poor areas in Africa and India whom they believed threatened their country's stability and their livelihood.

From the end of World War II into the late 1980s the US and its European allies confronted what they considered threats to democracy that came from the dictatorships of Russia and China. The buildup of nuclear weapons on both sides threatened the demise of civilization, but also may have saved a conflagration because everyone knew that the next war would be the last. In the meantime these dictatorships continued to expand their influence – sometimes by invasion of smaller countries – which the Western countries often confronted.

In the United States in the 1960s and 1970s, Americans were warned about the need to win the war in Vietnam to stop the spread of "godless communism" which had its roots in China. Americans were told by their leaders that the war was being won as it became a hopeless quagmire. Massive protests erupted across the US and many young men resisted the military draft or fled to Canada to avoid it. But eventually the fallacy of the possibility of winning this war was exposed. Years later China and Vietnam because major trading partners of the US.

A constitutional crisis erupted when the rule of law was threatened after President Richard Nixon participated in the cover-up – and possible planning – of a burglary at the headquarters of the Democratic Party in 1972. Nixon resisted the inquiry into this crime and eventually fired the special prosecutor who investigated. The Supreme Court insisted that Nixon turn over tapes of his conversations that may have implicated him, and he chose to resign rather than disobey the order of the court. Democracy was temporarily saved, at least in the US.

When Ronald Reagan became the US President in 1981, inflation had gotten out of control beginning in the late 1970s and the nation sought stability. He played tough with those he characterized as hostile to American interests both inside and outside of the nation. He cut taxes, which benefited primarily the wealthiest Americans, and reduced many domestic programs. His policies lead to a greatly increased national debt, which ultimately slowed the economy that was inherited by his Vice President, George H. W. Bush, when he became President.

When Reagan took office, the US was the world's largest lending nation. When he left office, the US was the world's largest debtor. This was the beginning of an era of borrowing to finance the lifestyle of Americans that led to increased debt on the generations that followed – with only the interest paid and the principle continuing to build. Those left holding the bag for the diminished economy in the long-term were those who paid the bulk of taxes, that is, the middle class, while the wealthiest continue to give themselves tax breaks that they then loan back to the government with interest.

At the same time that Reagan was in office, Margaret Thatcher became the first female Prime Minister of Britain. Her policies emphasized deregulation of the financial sector, privatizing state owned companies, and similarly to Reagan, reducing the influence of trade unions.

The Soviet Union – composed of Russia and a number of satellite nations – collapsed in the early 1990s due to a realization by its leaders that it had become unwieldy and that they could not dictate progress to its people who had no personal incentive to contribute to the economy.

A brief experiment with democracy then began in Russia and other former Soviet nations. But soon after the Soviet collapse, many of the valuable assets of Russia fell into the hands of previous government officials, creating a new class of billionaires and an oligarchy, with Vladimir Putin as Russia's first elected president. Putin soon took over control of the courts and threatened journalists who reported on his actions. He confiscated the assets of oligarchs who opposed him, some of whom wanted the country to move toward greater democracy.

Bill Clinton ran for US President in 1992 on the motto: "It's the economy, stupid," and won because a majority voted to end the Reagan/Bush economic slowdown. When he became President he raised taxes, after which the country was able to reduce its debt and the economy took off. But Clinton also weakened the standing of many at the lower end of the economic scale by ending "welfare as we know it." He then signed Republican-sponsored legislation in 1999 to rescind key provisions of the Glass-Steagall Act that had been put in place to protect bank deposits after the Great Depression.

George W. Bush took over as US President in 2001 and soon enacted a trillion dollar tax cut that mainly benefitted the rich. This stimulated the economy temporarily, but once again increased the national debt. He united the country after the attacks on the New York World Trade Towers in September of that year and reminded the country that the enemy is not Muslims, but those who hold hateful ideologies. He also committed substantial funds to the relief of AIDS in Africa and had a diverse cabinet. But his popularity plummeted after run-away speculation in real estate and stocks fueled by too much loose money created a bubble that burst into the biggest economic downturn since the Great Depression. He put a $700 billion stimulus packet in place that did little to turn the economy upright because the funds mainly were pumped into large banks.

Barack Obama was elected and took over in 2009 amidst this historic downturn. The $747 billion American Recovery and Reinvestment stimulus package that he put into place also was slow to show returns but the economy recovered, and ultimately did well, under his presidency. He championed equal pay for women, health care for poor families, increased grants for low income students, and appointed two women to the US Supreme Court. He signed the Hate Crimes Prevention Act regarding violence based on sexual orientation and repealed the "Don't Ask, Don't Tell" policy for the military. He fostered new regulations on factories and power plants to slow global warming. The Affordable Care Act extended health insurance to millions that were previously uninsured. He negotiated a deal with Iran in 2015 to limit their production of nuclear weapons. But he failed to prosecute those whose speculation and fraudulent practices led to the Great Recession.

Beginning with Spain in 2005, same-sex marriage was allowed in a number of Western nations, culminating in its legalization by a US Supreme Court decision in 2015.

In much of the world, populist leaders who overthrew the established order replaced it with themselves and their supporters, rather than establishing a true democratic government. Examples of popular revolt abound in history, but its successes in establishing real democracy have been few. Oppressive governments that have been challenged by popular movements often have yielded to more oppression or civil war. Countries that took a slower path toward becoming democratic were more successful, including England, France and the US.

Popular revolts in Central and South America usually resulted in governments run primarily for the wealthy, although Mexico was able to establish a political system that was largely democratic. Venezuela, which deteriorated to the point of near mass starvation, provided provisions to those who were willing to vote for the current president in its charade of democracy.

Egypt, where the Arab Spring started in 2011, once again regressed to a dictatorship, while other nearby countries, such as Libya and Syria became caught in civil wars that went on for years.

Some areas of Africa that attempted revolution or tried to move toward democracy have regressed to one-man rule, many with mass starvation. The "Democratic Republic" of the Congo, which was supported in its move toward independence by Belgium in 1960, quickly reversed into chaos. Random slaughter between tribes is a regular occurrence in many African countries, where the wealthy support themselves on a country's vast natural resources while millions starve.

In Western Europe, countries that had hopes of establishing real democracy have seen it deteriorate. In Germany adherents of Nazism have doubled over the last ten years. In France, neo-Nazis are a genuine presence in elections. In Italy, a right wing populist party has gained ascendency. And in Britain, a measure to leave the European Union passed when framed in anti-immigration rhetoric.

The 2016 presidential election extended "populism" to the US that already had erupted in Europe. But "the People" favored by those voters included only their own segment of the population, based on ethnic, economic, or party divisions. A populist revolt by those who believed themselves financially vulnerable catapulted Our Leader into the presidency. What got him there was a promise to overhaul what his followers believed to be a government that ignores them. He was elected on a pledge to "make America great again," which meant, for his followers, a resurrection of an America they once knew – where they could pursue the American Dream. He was elected despite describing Mexicans as "rapists and murders," and proposing to ban all Muslims from the country.

Under the first year of the new President, the US and world economy grew at a steady pace. Congress passed few laws, but in December, 2017, cut taxes substantially, primarily for corporations and the most wealthy.

In 2018, a probe by a Special Counsel into possible corruption in the 2016 election widened with indictments of some of the President's former aids in a plot to upend the election with Russian involvement. The President's comment was that the Special Counsel probe is "an attack on our country."

In the last two hundred years the light of democracy spread around the world due to cooperation – often between rivals – despite the many who have tried to establish authoritarian governments. Western democracies experienced a level of prosperity never before known. But this prosperity gave way to chronic greed by those who believe that they never can have a big enough piece of the pie. The results have consumed our lives and economies. It is the loss of this struggle against greed that has led to the downfall of democracy.

HOW WE FAILED

We now have lost democracy – in the United States and throughout the world.

I keep asking myself what went wrong. What were we thinking? What could "We the People" have done to keep our democracy in place?

I guess we just stopped paying attention.

We were busy – with our jobs, our children, and other obligations that seemed to take up the passing hours of our lives. We relied on political parties and leaders to keep our democracies strong. We thought we'd vote and contribute to those who seem to represent our values and that everything would be just fine. But we totally lost track of what those values even are.

As I look over the past few years, I am amazed at how we let democracy slip out of our grasp.

It all seems obvious now. All the warnings were there: the gradual deterioration of human rights around the world; the movement everywhere toward greater degradation of others; the attitude of many of us that we and our needs are superior to others; a loss of tolerance for differences between us; refusing to recognize each other as valid human beings; the abandonment of the democratic concept that what is good for one is good for all. Perhaps most importantly, we failed to have a conversation about our essential democratic values, how to maintain them, and how we can apply these principles to our world, including the diverse group of people that make it up. As we let our values deteriorate, democracy disappeared right before our eyes.

In Ancient Greece and in the early days of our modern democracies – including the US, France and England – we once discussed our most important values. We knew we wanted to overthrow oppression and replace it with a more democratic way of life. We knew that we wanted to be valued as human beings. The most essential of these values was that if we are to retain human rights for some it must be maintained for all, and if any of us lose our basic rights then all are threatened. This is the essence of the concept of the rule of law – rather than domination by an individual or a few – that we knew was essential to making democracy work.

But early in our history we lost the idea that democracy is truly government by and for the People, that is, all of the people. We started to think that if our own interests were met then that was good enough. Of course others thought the same about themselves and their groups that were made up of those of their race, religion, gender, sexual identity, and political views. We forgot that maintaining our rights requires that the rights of all are respected.

As time went on we assumed that our basic democratic structure always would be there. We could just live our lives as we pleased and somehow a guarantee was built into our society that would protect us. And so we failed to think about our role in creating the world we want to live in and just followed those who seemed to know better. We neglected to clarify our democratic vision and how to maintain it.

We turned our heads and failed to pay attention as our most essential democratic values were forgotten and eventually lost. This is what led to the end of our noble experiment. We neglected our responsibilities as participants in democracy in a number of ways.

Raising Responsible Children

As we moved toward a culture that no longer truly honors democracy, even in our so-called democratic countries, children rarely were raised to make responsible choices. Rather than gradually introducing greater choice and responsibility, parents made most major life decisions for their children, who failed to develop the judgment and skills needed for the functioning of democracy. Our children did not develop an ability to identify and work with others toward mutually beneficial goals.

Democracy's most essential theme is that the success of a nation and everyone in it is intertwined. Thus where children are encouraged to be the best version of themselves they also learn to support the success of others. But our democracies turned into places where competition is honored over cooperation, where children are taught that their responsibility is to themselves and those like them rather than to their society as a whole. We failed to teach them how to make democracy work by practicing interpersonal respect and cooperation.

As parents, we neglected to emphasize the true democratic values that promote what is best for "We the People." We trained our children to act as if they can advance themselves in a way that ignores the needs of others, which is impossible. The predictable result has been a great polarization and the crumbling of our society.

We have failed in the most basic tenet of democratic child raising, which is to help children develop essential decision-making skills and to make choices that allow them to experience the consequences of their decisions while keeping them safe. Thus most of our children never developed the ability to make the responsible decisions needed to maintain our democracies, or to learn how best to act in a way that honors all those of which our societies are composed.

Education

In our schools we failed to teach children how to think but instead taught them what to think. We trained them to do all they can to get ahead of others, rather than to collaborate toward common goals. Children in democracies became excellent at doing what they were told rather than determining their own paths or thinking about right and wrong, and how these values affect their real lives. We rarely taught them to identify and work with others toward what it takes to make society work.

Our schools became factories for training children to think only of their own needs, while leaving others to fend for themselves. This turned out to be not only impractical but impossible, because people cannot succeed in the real world by themselves. When the time came to stand up for democracy, our citizens were ill-prepared to defend it because they had never thought about its importance to their lives.

Economics

Distancing ourselves from others rather than including them in our society's growing prosperity became an obsession for those who continued to pull away economically. Despite the Western nations being the richest in history, we built walls between ourselves and others both within and outside of our countries – literally and figuratively.

There were many whose families had lived for generations in democratic countries who felt that they were left out of the increasing prosperity. We failed them as a society by neglecting to provide training and job opportunities in new skills. Most of those who prospered in Western nations looked only after their narrow self-interests, which ultimately met the needs of no one when funds failed to circulate and our economies collapsed.

In the US we created continually larger wealth and income gaps between the richest and the rest of us by giving huge tax breaks to those who needed them least, and leaving those who needed breaks struggling to catch up. Meanwhile, we accumulated substantial national debt which put a burden on everything we tried to do as a society, including providing roads, bridges, and schools. We did this in the 1980s, in the early 2000s, and again in 2017. This repeated pattern had predictable results – our national debt grew and 90% of the population continued to fall further behind, while paying back the debt fell mainly on them. As their financial situation deteriorated, many voted for politicians who promised to make their country great again. Those who were elected only tightened the screws by again cutting taxes on the wealthy, leaving a growing long-term debt burden, and then claiming a need to reduce health and retirement benefits.

Healthcare

The idea that some people can have healthcare coverage while others lack it never has worked. Many diseases cannot be contained unless everyone is protected in such areas as tuberculosis, flu epidemics, and childhood diseases which now are on the rise. Emergency rooms are overburdened with those who must be seen but cannot pay for services.

Providing insurance for some members of the population ultimately is more expensive than providing it for everyone because about a quarter of the expense of private insurance, which should go to medical benefits, instead goes to denying medical care. In most Western European countries – plus Canada, Japan, and others – everyone is covered, which makes the administration of medical care much easier and cost effective. No one should need to be concerned about whether they qualify. In the US, the richest country on earth, life expectancy continues to decline as a large segment of the population is denied medical care. Lack of insurance in the US alone is responsible for over 30,000 deaths per year.

The Environment

Our environment – including the natural world around us – is our source of life. As we have polluted and destroyed our world we also have threatened our own existence.

As we increased the carbon in our atmosphere the earth warmed, melting polar ice caps and raising the level of the oceans that shrunk our land mass and threatened coastal cities everywhere.

We have made our air harder to breathe and shortened the lives of many by increasing respiratory distress, especially for children, who are the most vulnerable. We have polluted our water in the name of progress, which has negatively affected the health of millions. We have allowed a poisoning of our soil with pesticides and fertilizers, and this has negatively affected those creatures of nature that support our planet, such as bees. This also has interrupted our own lives and reproductive cycles, leading to increased cancers and intellectual disabilities.

Worst of all, we have scarred our planet extensively to allow large corporations to profit at the expense of the many. This is the antithesis of the most fundamental principles upon which our democracies were founded.

Science

The main purpose of science no longer is to serve the needs of the People, but rather, to control them.

Electronic spying to ensure that the daily activities of citizens support the State has become the main focus of scientific research. Exploring the universe, prolonging life, and making living easier for the multitudes no longer is a priority now that democracy is dead. The desire of leaders to control the People far outweighs any efforts to benefit them. It now is the role of all members of society to contribute their efforts to support the State. We are, of course, told that this is for the benefit of all because the State only exists to serve us. All are forced to tow that political line, but few believe it.

Most scientific research now focuses on controlling how people lead their lives. The People are the State, and the State is the People, we are told, and therefore it is up to citizens to do all within their power to keep the State strong.

The World of Politics

We have overturned representative democracy and replaced it with rulers who see the role of people as serving them. They do this while claiming to serve the higher purpose of doing what works best for the People.

Running for office in our democracies became an extremely expensive process and successful politicians usually were supported by large corporations who expected – and received – a return on their investments.

Voters who thought they were supporting leaders who would look after their interests ended up with democratically elected autocrats who gradually consolidated their power in Western countries, ignoring the interests of individuals who supported them. They became masters at serving only a gradually narrower segment of the population, eventually concentrating power only in themselves and those close to them. They also packed the courts with judges who backed oligarchic government.

In nations such as China and Russia, revolutions long-ago led to authoritarian rule under the guise of establishing the voluntary Communist state central to Marxism. Of course that voluntary state never has come about.

Politics essentially has died in the West as the

oligarchs who now rule that part of the world need no longer justify their actions to maintain themselves in power. Instead, they bring into power only those who support their oppressive regimes. There no longer is a need to operate nations on democratic principles. The main role of the State is to keep a grip on the People and prevent them from ever again initiating revolution based on democratic ideals.

THE ENABLERS

THROUGHOUT HISTORY, and no doubt into pre-history, there have been those who have supported their leaders and those who have rebelled. There always have been people who thought they knew how to run things better than those at the top, or simply wanted to replace them.

With the advent of agriculture, about ten thousand years ago, our ancestors went from being members of wandering tribes to creating permanent settlements. These settlements eventually enlarged into cities and then states. Membership in a stable state was more likely to result in long-term survival than the wandering lifestyle of hunter-gatherers.

Members of states were required to support it by taxation, joining the military, and following its laws and customs.

It is impossible to know when democratic elements were introduced into the earliest states, but the most famous case of ancient times was that of Athens. There was a degree of democracy in ancient Rome, allowing some people to become citizens. After that, democratic elements slowly worked their way into the Western world, starting in England with the introduction of the Magna Carta in 1215, and culminating with the establishment of the American republic by the thirteen colonies that rebelled against England in 1775.

As its Constitution states, the United States was established on the principle of the sovereignty of "We the People." This principle came out of a long evolving idea in the Western world that recognized people as worthwhile entities to be respected. As more people became educated, they contributed to the functioning and improvement of the State.

This slowly replaced the idea that people should remain subservient to the upper classes, although this did remain the case in Russia and most countries of the East.

Slowly the idea of rule of law – a society governed by laws rather than the whims of its rulers – gained ground in the West, beginning in England. This made the eventual introduction of democracy possible. But there always have been those who supported powerful people or political parties over democratic principles and believed that democracy is not practical nor possible. Most people were likely to support those they saw as acting in their own interests or those of their group, rather the interests of the people as a whole. An education about, and understanding of, democratic principles among the people was rare. But when people were educated about how democracy benefits everyone they were more likely to support it.

Establishing democratic principles always has been a challenge. In England, there was a struggle between those who wanted to maintain the monarchy and those who wanted to depose it for hundreds of years. At the beginning of the United States there were many who did not trust democracy. Most had never seen it work, having lived their lives under a monarchy. Some entertained the notion of making George Washington king. In France, after their Revolution, power alternated between a republic and monarchy for 80 years. In Russian and China, domination by strong leaders eventually destroyed the democratic aspirations of their revolutions.

There are a number of stages that most revolutions go through. Before revolution there is strong resentment among much of the population against rule that is seen to be repressive. Next, an underground organizing movement takes place that eventually results in an above ground open revolt. If successful, a new government is put in place. But after that, a lack of unified vision among leaders of exactly how to replace the old system often results in the installment of a regime that is just as repressive or worse.

The American Revolution was a rare example of a situation where leaders first saw their democratic vision falter, as it did under the Articles of Confederation, but then were able to work together to forge a new and more viable nation. All members of the Constitutional Convention of 1787 were not united in their vision. It took four months to create a document to govern the new nation and all admitted that the resulting compromise was far from perfect. Delegates were torn over divisive issues such as slavery. Nevertheless, they forged a document that embraced the basic principle of human dignity that "All Men are Created Equal," even though that dignity was denied to women, slaves and Native Americans.

The main principle behind the Constitution was that all are equal before the law and no one is above anyone else. Three branches of government were put in place to keep each other from abusing their powers. Yet throughout the history of the

US, and of all Western nations, the partisan alignment of government officials often have threatened democracy itself. Members of Congress often have represented only the concerns of their own constituents or financial supporters. Judges have acted upon narrow prejudices (supporting slavery at one time), and presidents often have represented only that segment of the population which they have seen as in line with their political views.

Although the term "democracy" was used by many in the Western nations to describe the principle behind their government, few actually had a clear concept about what democracy really means and how to sustain it. If it means "government by the People," exactly what is meant by "the People?" Should leaders in democracies be loyal to parties and leaders or to "the People" themselves, and how would that look?

For most people, their parties and financial supporters are much more visible, and therefore more worthy of loyalty, than an abstract idea like democracy. The workings of a democracy – with its emphasis on the common good rather than benefits to one individual or group – are hard for most people to fathom. Thus allegiance to a dominant leader is an easy trap for most people to fall into.

The strong leaders of history are those who have, in many ways, moved civilization forward. Alexander the Great, Genghis Khan, and Charlemagne were among those who attracted immense followings. Their followers saw greatness in themselves through their leaders despite their ruthless treatment of conquered peoples they considered less human than themselves.

In the history of democratic states, it is those most committed to the common good who were the heroes, such as George Washington, Winston Churchill and Franklin Roosevelt. Opposing them were the anti-heroes of the democratic era – King George III, Adolph Hitler and Benito Mussolini. King George ruled uneasily in an emerging democratic state. Hitler and Mussolini were

democratically elected before they assumed absolute power.

In the Germany and Italy of the 1930s there
was a growing number of followers who enabled
leaders with strong personalities to move their
nations from democracy to autocracy. The trick of
these leaders was to appeal to those who believed
their promise that they would make their countries
great again. Their enablers joined their personality
cults as they abandoned democracy by calling for a
glorious utopian future that only included the dominant ethnic group. We now can look back and see
how, in these countries, democracy was doomed.

This pattern repeated in our times. Once the
dominant members of society believe that they or
their groups are more deserving than others, and
establish a government based on that principle, it is
hard to reverse course even when they and their own
group becomes marginalized. Vladimir Putin was
democratically elected, but moved toward absolute
authority by overpowering the Russian legislature

and courts, and abolishing the free press. He attacked everyone who opposed him. But he only was able to assume autocratic power as his growing band of enablers supported him in doing so. In China, which once maintained a façade of being a democracy, its leader has declared himself President for Life, again supported by his many enablers.

We have seen a pattern of elected presidents establish oppressive regimes – often fueled by claims of ethnic superiority – in over a dozen modern nations. They all have come to power – and then consolidated their hold – by promising their followers that they would rid them of failed past leaders while building a better future. Before long they concentrated their power as they themselves became the oppressors. A brief list of democracies turned authoritarian includes Russia, Syria, Turkey, Venezuela, Poland, Hungary, South Africa, and now, the United States.

Each step on the way to establishing authoritarian government is a test. First, the future

authoritarian is elected on a platform of return-
ing greatness to his country by helping those who
have fallen behind, and purging, or threatening to
purge, those who are blamed for economic stagna-
tion. Then he slowly consolidates power, bringing
more followers into line, questioning the patriotism
of those who doubt him. Lastly, he takes power over
all aspects of the country, attacking those who stand
in the way of the move toward "greatness," including politicians, the press, and anyone who dares to
express an independent voice. All along the way his
enablers slowly back off from speaking out about
these practices that they once saw as dangerous,
until they become caught in a web of moral ambi-
guity from which there is no return.

In the United States, Our Leader was legitimately elected in 2016. As in all modern countries
that have lost their democracies, his election was
fueled by a promise to lift his followers. Like all
the others, he promised to make his country great
while denigrating those he claimed were holding

the country back. And as happened with the others, many who once opposed his rants against minorities and democracy joined the ranks of his enablers, worshipping at his feet and becoming a part of his personality cult while abandoning democracy altogether.

His enablers created alternative stories to distract the public from the investigation into collaboration between Our Leader and Russia to steal the election, such as calling it politically motivated or a hoax. Congressional cowardice, along with his enablers in the media, were the chief contributors to the demise of democracy in the US. If, as in the fable of *The Emperor's New Clothes*, the President said that up is down or black is white, his enablers still would have backed him.

DEMOCRACY'S DEATH

DEMOCRACY ONCE WAS A VISION of respect for all people that we somehow let slip out of our sight. This vision became established in many nations, only to be reversed, sometimes by coup, but recently by legitimately elected leaders. In our day the best way to overthrow democracy is to establish an authoritarian government in its name.

It's easy to feel guilty now that democracy is lost. We all keep asking, away from the eyes and ears of the authorities, how we could let this happen. Now we see, in retrospect, that we didn't really learn from history. The signs all were there; we should have seen this coming.

Around the world early in this century, many democratically elected leaders gradually shifted greater power to themselves, undermining legislators, the courts, the press and every other check that was meant to represent the will of the People.

There are many who believe that democracy is not the best form of government. And considering that authoritarian governments have been established in its name, who are we to doubt them?

When people don't live in turbulent times or places, they are content to let others do their thinking. Occasionally going to the polls in the midst of our busy lives seems like enough of a burden. But only when we feel threatened – as individuals or nations – do we pay attention, and then we once again settle back into complacency after the crisis passes.

In the United States, the 2001 attacks on the World Trade Center unified Americans in a feverish desire to defeat the enemy, and the financial crisis of 2008 motivated people to go to the polls to remove the politicians they considered responsible for the threat to their financial security.

Once, democracies died as the result of military coups. This happened during the cold war in places such as Argentina, Brazil, Peru, Guatemala, Greece, Pakistan and Ghana. But more recently many legitimately elected leaders gradually assumed greater authority, leading to an overthrow of democracy around the world. It wasn't clear until recently how these events were connected.

In Venezuela, Hugo Chavez, who claimed to be the true representative of his people, was elected in 1998. He slowly undermined the power of the courts and elected representatives. As his power waned in 2003, he stalled a popular referendum, repressing challengers to his authority. After his death in 2013, Chavez was followed in the presidency by Nicolas Maduro, who imprisoned the country's major opposition leader. The current government, despite extreme oppression, barely has control of the economy. Food shortages and poverty rule, despite a massive oil infrastructure. In a recent election, bags of rice were exchanged for votes. Food – and democracy – no longer trickles down to the level of the people.

In Russia, Vladimir Putin undermined every democratic institution soon after being elected in 2000. Russia now is ruled by its oligarchs, with Putin at the head. The owner of an independent TV station who criticized the government was forced to flee the country. The billionaire head of the giant Yukos oil company was imprisoned in 2003 for ten years after financing opposition parties. Defectors from Russian spy agencies have been poisoned in other lands.

The president of Turkey, Recep Erdogan, has said "We are the People." He seized the assets of sponsors of an opposition political party in 2004. A cartoonist who lampooned Erdogan in 2005 went to prison. He has accused journalists of spreading terrorism and sued news organizations that have criticized him, forcing them to be sold to government-backed organizations. A government attack on protesters against corruption in 2013 resulted in 22 deaths. A 2016 failed coup led to a purge of 100,000 state officials, closed newspapers, and resulted in over 50,000 arrests, including judges and journalists. A 2017 referendum, of which the results likely were fraudulent, gave sweeping powers to Erdogan.

Numerous nations in Africa have had their constitutions changed to replace democratic elections and award their once-revolutionary leaders with the presidency for life. Four of Africa's leaders have been in power for more than 35 years due to constitutional amendments, in Zimbabwe, Angola, Cameroon, and Uganda. The results of oppression in these and other African countries have been violent rebellions, with the deaths of thousands and the displacement of millions.

Countries of Western Europe also have shown themselves vulnerable to takeover by anti-democratic "populist" movements.

Voters in Great Britain approved an exit from the European Union in 2016 by a narrow margin. Anti-immigrant politicians convinced voters that they were losing jobs and were subject to increasing terrorist attacks due to an influx of immigrants. Those who voted for "Brexit" assumed that it would improve their job picture and economy. But membership in the European Union had included low trade barriers that actually created jobs and increased prosperity. The result of the vote is a lowered prospect for Britain's economy and a likely decrease, rather than increase, in employment.

In France, where a violent revolution once ended the monarchy, there has been a resurgence of the type of populism that seeks to benefit one part of the population at the expense of others. Marine Le Pen, the daughter of neo-Nazi holocaust denier Jean-Marie le Pen, now talks a more moderate line to attract voters to her right-wing, anti-immigrant, agenda. She lost the 2017 election after France's conservative leader, who opposed Le Pen's extreme views, recommended that voters elect the moderate Emmanuel Macron. After Macron's election, the extreme elements of the country seemed to slow their ascendance, but they remain a force.

After Germany's 2017 election, Angela Merkel, Chancellor since 2005, had a difficult time putting together a coalition due to the strong showing of opposition leaders, many of them anti-immigration. The authority of Merkel and other moderates was weakened, and those who opposed the European Union in Germany gained strength. As Europe's strongest economy, a weakening of Germany's leadership that favors open trade is seen by many as a threat to the economies of Europe.

In the United States, as in much of the world, there is a long tradition of making America safe for what some consider "real Americans," and less safe for those ethnically different from the majority. Although the country was forged as a "nation of immigrants," the human tendency to distrust those who look or act differently from themselves never has been far from the fore.

The US has a tradition of political mistrust that goes back to its earliest days. After its founders worked together to forge a constitution, the battle between proponents of greater and lesser central power began. The Federalists under John Adams, who wanted a stronger central government, opposed the new Democratic-Republican Party under Jefferson, which believed in limited government. Each saw the others as traitors to the ideals on which the country was founded. After putting aside their differences for four months to write the Constitution, neither side was willing to commit to working with the other to achieve national harmony based on the concept of "We the People" that they had forged.

As in other countries, patriotic fever always has peaked during challenging economic times when leaders inspired Americans to feel threatened, internally or externally, whether or not the threat was real.

In the 1830s, in defiance of the Supreme Court, Andrew Jackson used the Indian Removal Act to force the transfer of American Natives from their homes in the eastern states to reservations in the west. Among them were 15,000 Cherokee, about 4,000 of whom died on the journey. His excuse was a "threat" to the country from Native Americans.

In 1861, at the beginning of the American Civil War, the area around the US Capital was in danger of being overrun by rebels. Abraham Lincoln suspended habeas corpus, which requires that a defendant be brought before a judge to determine whether that person can be held. By law, habeas corpus only can be suspended by Congress.

In an expression of American imperialism, the US declared war on Spain in 1898, seizing Spanish territories from Cuba to the Philippines. This was supposedly in response to a threat by Spain against a much stronger United States.

In 1942, Japanese Americans were seen as a threat and interned not long after the attack on Pearl

Harbor by Japan. There was no evidence of collaboration in the attack on the part of those citizens.

In 2001, Americans recoiled after an attack that destroyed the World Trade Towers in New York City. The US went to war with the Al Qaeda attackers and their Taliban hosts in Afghanistan. Torture, or "enhanced interrogation," was used against "enemy combatants," which yielded no useful information, but sent a message that the US no longer respects international law that prohibits mistreatment of captives. This, of course, paves the way for the mistreatment of American captives.

One year later, Congress passed the USA Patriot Act that expanded the authority of the government to monitor phone and email communications, collect bank and credit reporting records, and track the activity of Americans on the Internet whether or not they were accused of a crime.

Before the 2016 election many Americans were unhappy with their lives financially and blamed the Federal government. Incomes, which had been going up in their families since World War II, were stagnating. The factories and plants where their families had worked were now closed or barely paying a living wage. They were stuck in jobs that guaranteed no future. They were unsure of how they ever would retire. They couldn't afford a college education for their children. Vacations were out of the question.

Many felt abandoned by the Democratic Party that their parents and grandparents had supported in the America of the 1940s, 50s, 60s, and 70s when their future seemed bright. But then factories closed and jobs went away. It seemed that no one cared, and the 2016 candidate of their parents' political party seemed to ignore them.

Then a man ran for president who promised that only he could fix it all. He would restore gainful employment. He would free the country from foreign domination. He would get rid of the immigrants who were stealing jobs. He would make America great again.

But for those who were paying attention, this

candidate presented danger signs to democracy that were obvious, including:

1. Disparaging everyone with whom he disagreed.
2. Disrespect for women.
3. Ignoring or firing advisors who suggested he act in keeping with democratic principles.
4. Attacks on the press.
5. Accusing those who had different political views of treason.
6. Support for dictators and strongmen around the world, including those in Russia, China, Hungary and the Philippines.
7. Nepotism – hiring his own family to run things because no one else could be trusted to push his extreme agenda.
8. Violating the emoluments clause of the US Constitution by profiting from his office.
9. Ignoring climate change and allowing destruction of the environment.

10. Removing governmental monitoring of poisons and toxins in food and water.
11. Saying whatever comes to mind and not thinking about the long-term consequences.
12. Threats of expulsion for immigrants.
13. Imposing the religion of the majority.
14. Denying the rights of sexual minorities.

The man who became the new President had grown up wealthy and was in the habit of making spot decisions for which there were no consequences. When he entered business he simply fired those who disagreed with him. His thrash and burn style was based on a viewpoint that whatever seemed the most expedient way to get through the next crisis was the best course. He went through numerous bankruptcies and lawsuits for breach of contract and paid to cover up sexual misconduct. He lost hundreds of millions of dollars but kept his businesses because of loans from dubious sources. In his business career he never gave serious consideration to the views of experts or of the long-term results of his behavior. He showed no interest in democratic management that brought together the best ideas of his advisors. Because of not learning to work well with others, his management style was more akin to the use of a sledgehammer than the scalpel of a skillful politician.

After the 2016 election things seemed to go well at first for the nation and the new President. The economy and markets continued the forward thrust of the previous administration. Enormous tax cuts were put into place by the Republican Congress at the end of his first year in office that seemed to spark growth. Despite continual disputes with many outside of his political party and many within, he was able to keep the loyalty of most of his electoral base due to continued promises to bring back prosperity to areas that had lost jobs in manufacturing, coal, and other industries, but that never happened.

He pulled out of the Paris environmental

accords which he claimed hurt jobs and threatened to leave NAFTA, a trade agreement with the two closest North American neighbors of the US. He made numerous attempts to repeal the Affordable Care Act of his predecessor despite its providing health care for tens of millions of Americans, but could not accomplish this even in a Republican Congress. He proposed to drastically cut benefits such as Medicaid, Social Security, and Medicare upon which many of his supporters depended. But he never put into place the massive infrastructure plan he promised that would improve roads and bridges while creating the jobs on which he based his campaign.

Because of his belligerent style and demands for loyalty, in a little over his first year in office the new President lost over two dozen close advisors and cabinet members including his Secretary of State, Secretary of Health and Human Services, Secretary of Veterans Affairs, National Security Advisor, Deputy Security Advisor, Press Secretary, and Chief of Staff. There was a continuing revolving door, with departures of those who dared to challenge his views or express concern about his outbursts. He only could bear to have "yes" men and women around him.

More tellingly, he continued to express views that disparaged those he considered enemies of the State, including Hispanic immigrants and those of the Muslim religion. He got many of his ideas for major decisions from one television station and called the other stations fake news.

At one time in US history major news stations tried to be objective, but more recently some have backed politicians or parties regardless of whether their actions were in keeping with democracy. This contributed to a polarization among Americans rather than an ability to determine whose actions contributed to – or detracted from – the good of the country.

As the US entered the second year of his administration, many hoped that this president's tantrums and poorly-conceived policies would begin to ease as advisors brought a more long-term, rational perspective. These expectations never were fulfilled as he continued his rants against those he considered threats, rather than discussing what might be the soundest policy with his advisors.

Throughout his presidential campaign and into his first term in office, the new President encouraged violence. He urged his followers to beat up protesters at his campaign appearances. During a march of white supremacists in Charlottesville, Virginia, a counter-protester was run down and killed. He refused to condemn the white supremacists, saying that there were "good people on both sides."

Numerous protests followed him for his first year in office, which included a Women's March in January, 2017, a Day without Immigrants in February of that year, a March for Science in April, and protests following his DACA decision in September. But after that the pace of protests slowed.

As many autocrats before him – and like those

in the countries previously mentioned – the new President stated his belief that the civil liberties of those who he considered his enemies should be curtailed. He said repeatedly that he wanted a special prosecutor to investigate his chief rival in the 2016 election. He threatened the owners of the newspapers that reported on the details of many of his scandals, including a possible conspiracy with Russia to spread false information that could sway the election. In November, 2017, he stated: "I'm the only one that matters," when asked about 450 State Department vacancies in positions needed to interact with foreign governments. He complained about the "massive" size of some federal agencies.

The stock market continued to improve for the first three years of his new presidency, fueled largely by the tax cuts given to the wealthy. But the bottom half of the population continued to fall further behind. Then the markets began to waver. The President declared that due to our trade deficits with other countries, particularly China, he would impose new tariffs. He addressed the concerns of many economists that these actions might start a trade war by stating that the country actually could win a trade war, despite the clear declaration by many experts on the right and left that there are no winners in trade wars.

Then a surprising trend developed in a number of 2018 US special elections. Areas that had supported the President – some by a large margin – voted to put Democrats in office both at the state and national levels. This happened in Alabama, where an accused child molester who had the support of the President was defeated, in Pennsylvania, where a conservative Democrat won by a small margin, and in Wisconsin, where a state Democratic Supreme Court candidate won a seat after declaring that "People are tired of special interests ruling and want to speak up." This seemed to be a growing trend across the US – voters seeing Republican candidates as representing the rich and powerful and not "We the People" as advertised.

The President refused to listen to his advisors and continued on a path of excoriating and firing those who did not fall in line with his way of thinking; of insulting minorities; of making up his own facts; and ignoring that his support was the lowest of any president after one year in office.

Not all of the President's actions were against the best interests of the People, but many were so inconsistent with his other actions that they had no real effect or meaning. After a massacre of 17 Florida high school students, he declared that he would support major changes in gun laws, but soon lost interest and changed his mind. After setting a deadline for the renewal of the DACA program that would have allowed young adults who arrived as children to stay in the US, he declared that "DACA is dead." After insulting the leader of North Korea, he switched and decided to negotiate on nuclear arms.

Federal Agents began targeting immigration activists in addition to immigrants themselves.

Despite a declared policy of only deporting criminals, illegal immigrants who were found were held for deportation, which was justified by the excuse that they were criminals just by being in the country. This included those who lived and worked in the US for decades while paying taxes and building lives with American spouses and children. The President's "zero tolerance" policy toward immigration resulted in the separation of families and deaths of immigrant children.

His inconsistencies and attacks on others made it clear to a growing number of voters that the President actually had no idea in what direction he wanted to lead the country. He campaigned on "draining the swamp," that is, getting rid of the heavy influence of large corporations and the wealthy on Washington, but those he hired to head numerous agencies often were opponents of the mission of the agencies they were expected to oversee, including the Environmental Protection Agency, Department of Energy, and the Consumer

Financial Protection Bureau. He continued to deny climate change even as the poles melted.

In March of 2018, the President announced that he had agreed to meet with the leader of North Korea, Kim Jong-un, with whom he had previously engaged in verbal attacks. The purpose of the meeting would be for the two leaders to discuss a possible decrease in nuclear weapons and reducing strife by continued negotiations between their representatives in the future.

He then broadcast some clarity about his true intentions, for those who paid attention, as he flirted with dictators. After stating his approval for the ruler of China when he declared himself President for Life, and supporting the President of the Philippines in ignoring the rule of law to kill those who commit drug crimes, he called Vladimir Putin to congratulate him on his fraudulent re-election as President of Russia. He then invited Putin to meet him in Finland in July, where they held private conversations with only translators allowed.

He never admitted the proven facts, even believed by many Republicans, that Russia had interfered in the 2016 election.

As the 2018 mid-term elections approached it became clear that candidates of the Democratic Party would become the new majority in the US House of Representatives. Many Republicans stated that they would not run for their seats to avoid the embarrassment of defeat, including Paul Ryan, speaker of the House. This raised the likelihood that impeachment proceedings would be initiated against the President for a number of possible reasons, including the Emoluments Clause of the Constitution (profiting from his office), obstructing justice for firing the head of the FBI (which the President admitted he did because of the Russia probe), and for obstructing investigations into his actions.

Over the next two years, the rights of citizens to protection from government intrusion under the US Constitution were greatly curtailed. A compliant Senate packed the courts with ideologues more committed to supporting the President's agenda than the rule of law.

The Report on the Investigation into Russian Interference in the 2016 Presidential Election, initiated and supervised by members of the President's political party, was released to the public in April, 2019. It clearly implicated the President and members of his campaign in meeting with Russians to affect the 2016 election, and confirmed that the President sought to obstruct the investigation. Again, the Republican-led Senate ignored those actions that clearly were illegal and violated the principle of the US Constitution that no one is above the law.

This encouraged the President in ever-greater excesses. He and his advisors defied subpoenas for records and testimony from Congress in the continued investigations into possible corruption. He ignored orders of judges to hand over his financial records and, with the help of a compliant Attorney

General, opened an investigation into those who had investigated him and his campaign.

This was the beginning of the end of democracy throughout our world, although few knew it. Almost no one believed that a totally authoritarian government could move into place so quickly considering the long history of the US democracy.

Once the results came in after the November 2020 election, the President was defeated soundly in both the popular and electoral votes. It became clear that a majority of Democrats would maintain control of the House of Representatives and possibly the Senate after being inaugurated in January. But, as he had done in 2016, the President insisted that the election had been rigged and that he actually had won both votes by large majorities.

Right after the election, the President announced that Vladimir Putin would visit the United States in late November. He also stated that he would have a major announcement for the American people at that time.

Many speculated about what that announcement would be, coming from a president about to leave office. Would the US and its previous rival agree at last to a nuclear test treaty? Would they create a plan to work for peace in some of the most tumultuous areas of the world, such as Africa and the Middle East? Or would the President's statement simply be a final tirade against the many people he considered his enemies?

During Putin's visit there was the usual fawning by the President for the man who, despite years of cyber threats against the US, he never once criticized. When **The Announcement** came during a special television broadcast it was the shock of a lifetime to those who had expected much, as well as those who expected nothing, from this President.

"People of America," he began from a prepared statement, "due to the election fraud committed during our recent election on all decent Americans by the Democratic Party, which resulted in false results, I am forced to declare Martial Law over the

United States. Because of the totally criminal behavior of the Democrats, many are being rounded up and arrested. For the foreseeable future, you may address me as Our Leader, as can all people of the Western Hemisphere. From now on President Putin will be addressed as Our Leader by the people of Europe, and the President of China, Xi Jinping, will be addressed as Our Leader by the people of Asia. The leaders of all major world governments have been contacted by our representatives and have agreed to comply with our request to allow us to take the lead in saving democracy here in the United States and in the rest of the world. Thank you."

Because the constitutions of nearly all nations promise democracy, and few deliver it, it was not a big stretch for the leaders of Russia and China to expand their dictatorships in the name of democracy. In the United States, we also now have made the move from democracy to dictatorship in the name of democracy.

After **The Announcement** most Republicans

and some Democrats who had been enablers of Our Leader praised him for his role in saving democracy. Those who denounced the news were arrested. The Press was curtailed and elections were suspended. And thus, at the approach of the year 2021, we embark on a new world order that appears to be the beginning of the end for democracy as we know it. Most of us, in our private conversations, discuss the fact that Our Leader never previously mentioned democracy or his support for it. By calling this new dictatorship a democracy, Our Leader probably has eliminated the chance of real democracy ever being restored. But we must avoid having anyone hear our concern as there are spies everywhere, including on our electronic devices. We are reminded of the vengence of Stalin, who arrested and killed millions he thought threatened his authority

Those of us who must now live with the loss of democracy privately question what we could have done differently. Most of us never were engaged in preserving it and this is the consequence. We never could be bothered to have a conversation about the nature of democracy and which leaders best represent it. We never thought about what people should do to prevent a dictatorship. But, at last, this got our attention.

There are many ways in which we failed.

We failed to insist on maintaining our authority, as We the People, for how our democracies should be run. We gave our authority to others because we always were too busy and believed we were unqualified to take responsibility for running our own countries. We neglected to discuss the nature of democracy and our role in preserving it in our schools, workplaces, organizations, and governments. We failed to come to an understanding of what democracy looks like and how best to maintain it. We gave our authority to those who now run our world and who have taken away our freedoms. But we didn't imagine it would come to this.

Now I go into hiding. I think it only is a matter of time before they find me. Once I am locked away there will be no recourse because there no longer are checks or balances on the powers of the State. My chances of regaining my freedom will be nil because I wrote this little book. Hopefully someone in the future will find it and read it, only to discover that there once was a bright vision for real democracy – government by the People – that we let slip away.

Democracy was a dream that we glimpsed in the night yet neglected to bring to the light of day. It was an opportunity for freedom that knocked at our door, yet we failed to even get out of our chair to give it entry.

Our Leader wants to maintain the illusion of democracy to avoid any thoughts of rebellion. His enablers, who are more concerned with saving themselves than in saving democracy, will no doubt continue to help uphold that pretense.

Throughout history we have suffered when we divided ourselves from other people, but prospered as a society when we saw our welfare connected to that of others. This was the essence of the democracy we once had. When we emphasized what we had in common, our world was a better place; when we emphasized our differences, the world became much worse.

One final thought: democracy disappeared because we failed to treat others with the respect and dignity that we want from them. We became each other's enemies, spurred to hatred by those who led us to democracy's demise. But there really are no foes who brought this upon us, only our willingness to participate in the illusion that some are our enemies, rather than focusing on the realization of a common vision of government by "We the People" – all of the people.

We portrayed many of those around us – the "other" – as being on the opposite side of a barrier that we created as we ignored our common humanity.

And we failed to learn that the only real enemy is hate.

www.ingramcontent.com/pod-product-compliance
Lightning Source LLC
Chambersburg PA
CBHW030259030426
42336CB00009B/442